THE VERY SPECIAL
NIGHT

written by Ruth Shannon Odor

illustrated by Pat Karch

Sixth Printing, 1990

Nights are for resting and sleeping.

Some nights are quiet.

Some nights are stormy.

Some nights are dark.

Some are bright with a big moon and twinkling stars. Most nights are just ordinary. But some are very special.

One night, a night long, long ago, was
a special night—a very special night!

The town of Bethlehem was quiet that night. Almost everyone was asleep.

In the stable of an inn slept a man and a woman. The man was Joseph and the woman was Mary. They had to sleep in the stable. When they had come to Bethlehem that day, they had found the inn crowded.

In the same stable slept the cows

and the donkeys.

During the night a wonderful thing
happened! A baby was born to Mary. He
was a special baby. He was the Son of
God!

Mary wrapped the baby in soft
clothes. Then she laid Him on the soft
hay in the manger.

"I will name you Jesus," Mary said.
It was a very special night—a very
special night indeed!

That very same night, out on a hill near Bethlehem, shepherds were taking care of their sheep. To them this was the same kind of night as any other when they watched over their sheep and lambs.

Suddenly a bright light shone around them! And a bright and shining angel stood before them!

"Do not be afraid," said the angel. "I bring you good news—good news for everyone.

"Tonight in the city of Bethlehem, the Savior, Christ the Lord, is born! You will find Him wrapped in swaddling clothes and lying in a manger."

Then there were many angels praising God. They said, "Glory to God in the highest. And on earth peace, goodwill among men."

As quickly as they had come, the bright light and the angels were gone! Once more the night was dark and still. The shepherds were amazed.

"Let's go to Bethlehem," they said.

There they found Mary and Joseph
and baby Jesus!

On the way home, the shepherds
thanked God for what they had seen
and heard on that very special night.

At night, in a land far away, some wise men were looking at the stars in the sky. They saw a big, new star! It meant God's son was born!

How excited the wise men were! They planned a trip to the faraway land to find the baby, to worship Him, and to give Him gifts.

It was a very special night—that
night long ago—when Jesus was born.